A Job for the Dog

Written by Charlotte Guillain
Illustrated by Robert Dunn

Collins

Meet my dog Rocket.

He naps in my room.

I see a tail.

5

Rocket can be a cook.

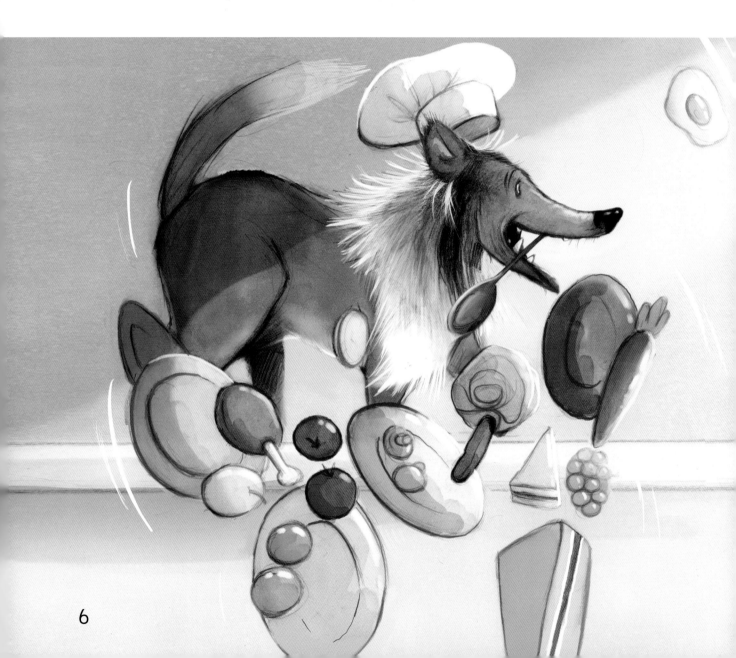

Rocket is not a good vet.

9

He can be a farmer.

Rocket digs up the seeds.

12

Rocket is a good dog.

The right job for Rocket

❖ After reading ❖

Letters and Sounds: Phase 3

Word count: 60

Focus phonemes: /ai/ /ee/ /igh/ /oo/ /oo/ /ar/ /or/ /ur/ /er/

Common exception words: my, he, you, I, be, no, the

Curriculum links: Understanding the World

Early learning goals: Reading: read and understand simple sentences; use phonic knowledge to decode regular words and read them aloud accurately; read some common irregular words

Developing fluency

- Your child may enjoy hearing you read the book.
- Take turns to read a page, but encourage your child to read all the speech bubbles. Remind them to think about how the girl is feeling and to look out for the exclamation marks so that they can read expressively.

Phonic practice

- Focus on the words with long vowels, beginning on pages 2 and 3. Ask your child which word has the /ee/ sound (*meet*) and which has the long /oo/ sound. (*room*)
- Ask your child to find the two letters that make each of these sounds on pages 10–12: /ar/ (*farmer*), /ee/ (*seeds*), /igh/ (*sigh*), /or/ (*for*).
- Challenge your child to find words with the long /oo/ or short /oo/ on pages 6–8. (*cook, food, good*) Ask your child to read the words aloud.

Extending vocabulary

- Ask your child:
  - Read the speech bubble on page 12. Can you **sigh**?
  - When might you sigh? (e.g. *when you can't go out because it is raining again, when there aren't any snacks in the kitchen*)
  - How do you feel when you sigh? (e.g. *disappointed, sad*)